Made in the USA
Monee, IL
21 February 2021

61047144R00073